Deer at Twilight

Poems from the North Cascades

D0958711

Paul J. Willis

STEPHEN F. AUSTIN STATE UNIVERSITY PRESS

Stephen F. Austin State University Press
PO Box 13007, SFA Station,
Nacogdoches TX. 75962.
sfapress@sfasu.edu

Book Design by: Emily Townsend
Cover Design by: Emily Townsend
Illustrations by: John Hoyte

ISBN: 978-1-62288-182-6
First Edition

To Christopher Norment
trail partner extraordinaire

CONTENTS

I.

II.

III.

He would speak of trees, from the cedar that is in Lebanon to the hyssop that grows in the wall; he would speak of animals, and birds, and reptiles, and fish.

—I Kings 4:33

1.

Mt Shuksan, WA

Snow Creek

(Oreamnos americanus)

A mossy flat, a rotting log, huckleberries
greening up under the lodgepole
next to the creek. What better place
to hover with a few stray mosquitoes
to regain a sense of where you are—
something Bill Bradley said about
being on a basketball court, but
here it is different, the only whistles
from hoary marmots, the only referee
the occasional mountain goat.

True, the goats can stare at you balefully,
reminding you of things you have done
and things you have left undone,
but now, in June, with the heat of summer
coming on, their fur has molted off
in patches to reveal their sagging skin,
and it is hard to take them seriously.

The creek, though, riffling its way
into and out of clear green eddies,
is something to pay attention to.
Just below you it flows down a steep slab
as effortlessly as, well, a mountain goat,
leaving its taste of cool and damp
like little tufts of ivory hair
caught on the needles of silver fir.

The Thing That Is Not

(Maianthemum racemosa)

Climbing out of Canyon Creek in September sun,
the ladder leaves of false Solomon's seal.
False. As if the flower does not measure up
to what it is supposed to be, and never will.
Known only by what it is not.

Shading all this falsity is Douglas fir—
a true positive, one would suppose,
named for the intrepid Scot who scoured
the Columbia Basin for plants and seeds
to diversify the British gardens of his betters.

But think of the scientific name,
Pseudotsuga menziesii, given
in honor of Archibald Menzies,
the botanist-surgeon who sailed along
with George Vancouver in 1792.

That part, sure. But *pseudotsuga*—that means
"pseudo-hemlock." As in, sort of like a hemlock,
but no. And that's not all.
Checking the index of my natural history guide
to the North Cascades, I discover

false bugbane, false chanterelle,
false lily-of-the-valley, false spikenard,
false miterwort. This habit of definition
de negativa has got to go,
in spite of its theological roots.

The church fathers—Augustine, Aquinas—
realized that God could only be described
by what he or she or it was not.
God is infinite, for example:
in other words, falsely finite.

But surely—a flower, a tree?
Can't we take them for what they are?
It's a little like calling a member of the Skagit tribe
non-white. Which, all too often, we do.
We, *kemo sabe?*

Flyaway

A fritillary, petite and orange,
    flits back and forth across the creek
        and lands on top of my blue pack.

How firmly it attaches its feet,
    waving it wings
        as if testing possibilities.

Little orange one, what if you
    carried my big blue pack
        just up the hill to the next meadow?

I'm sure there is something there
    for you—a late-summer flower
        that is your favorite.

Think of it as a tiny bit of conditioning,
    some weight training to get you ready
        to visit the monarchs in Mexico.

You could set it down,
    my big blue pack, in a small
        round campsite under a subalpine fir.

When I caught up, you could rest
    and watch me raise my tent,
        puzzling over the hooks and poles.

Then, when the sun goes down
    and the stars come out and
        I slip into my sleeping bag,

you could fold your wings
    beside my ear, and you
        would be welcome in my dreams.

Crater Mountain

Gary Snyder, I've dogged you here
from Matterhorn Peak in Yosemite.
Not much to show for your residence, though.
A concrete block inscribed with the date 1951.
A rusty shaft, topped with the hub of a fire-finder.
Tin cans spilling over the summit.
And lower down, a twisted cable atop the cliff
overlooking the old mule trail.

But the North Cascades still unroll
their mountains and rivers without end.
Desolation Peak to the north,
where beyond Jack Mountain would appear
the light of your friend Jack Kerouac,
whose fame in death eclipsed your own.
And Sourdough across Ross and Diablo Lakes,
where Philip Whalen lit his lamp in obscurity.

The pale ghost of a butterfly
lands beside me in the breeze.
Flies buzz. A motorcycle whines
from the highway, new since your time,
six thousand feet below,
passing the collapsed log ruin
by the creek of the guard station that once
held your bags of rice.

Tempus fugit—what can I say?
I lift a plug of twisted glass
and stow it in the back of my pack.
For me? For you? Me, I think—
your time is past and mine is soon getting there.
But what can be seen can be seen
through high still air.
Day after day after day.

Huckleberry Love Poem

(Vaccinium deliciosum)

Back in camp from Crater Mountain,
I plunge into a dark, clear pool
and climb out onto the shore.

While my body dries in September sun,
I take my pick of the huckleberries at my side—
huckleberries blue and round,
waiting under their fall red leaves.

And then I eat them, one by one,
so delicious, so full of pleasure,
naked as I am on the bank, tasting
again the golden age, when clusters
of grapes crushed themselves
against our ripe and innocent lips.

Away from you, dear, this is as close
as I can come to your sweet love.

And, given these berries—
as surely as Adam was given
the fruit his wife so cherished—
pretty darn close, actually.

Community

As I fire the stove for supper,
footsteps, a man with an ice ax
strapped to the back of his pack.
I have seen no one all day.

"Hello," I say. "On your way out?"
He looks serious, he keeps walking.
But he pauses and says, over his shoulder,
"It'll be dark before I get down."

"Did you climb something?" I persist.
"Jack," he says, as if it pains him
to speak again. And then he is gone,
before I can invite him to a cup of tea.

Not that he would have taken it.
But still, the chance of companionship—
it would have been worth it, just to try.
Otherwise, we might as well pull

factory shifts in the wilderness,
put our peaks on assembly lines.
Race to a summit, check it off,
and not a wasted word between us.

Devils Park Shelter

The path here is edged crimson
with the leaves of huckleberry,
and down by the creek the willow
is yellow. A cloud spreads across the sun
after weeks of perfect weather,
a suggestion of winter sure to come.
Not that this shelter would be much help
against sleet and snow—too many shakes
on the roof are gone or have shifted
marvelously askew. Still,
it is a thing of fallen beauty, poised
on the edge of a meadow that rises on and on
amid shapely stands of steepled fir,
far-flung churches of the mind.
And I'm glad the shelter is still here,
for some like it have been burned down
in compliance with the Wilderness Act,
fifty years old this month and counting.
The White Pass Shelter by Glacier Peak,
for example, visited by Gary Snyder
and Alan Ginsberg, was done to ashes
by a regretful trail crew
who sent them their apologies.
In the hour before Ginsberg died,
he set about building the shelter of a poem.
I guess I can understand that.

Bear Scat

Bear scat, you are the closest thing
I've had to company the last three days,
not counting the black-tailed deer
who licked my urine from the ground
at the last camp. Or the Douglas squirrels
chasing each other around the trunk
of a Douglas fir in a mating frenzy.
And a couple of owls, those decorous
hooters, along with the libidinous
whumpf of a grouse or two.
So, well, maybe I've had a few visitors.
But what is it with you guys? All about
shitting and pissing and fucking.
What makes you think
you're better than the rest of us?

Dry Creek

Dry Creek, that you are not.
  The trail walks a checkered log
across your rapids. Yesterday
  I stood in the snow where you began,
white as the foam that courses
  now through moss, through boulders,
under the cedars and the hemlock
  to the gray, impassive lake.

I think I am alone with you
  until a young man rounds the bend
above the crossing—one leg flesh
  and bone, one leg sprung steel—
and he treads the log without a pause.
  His pack appears to be no burden.
He is heading, he says
  to me, for Desolation.

Desolation Peak

Jack, I owe you an apology. Some years
ago I left a note on Matterhorn Peak:
Jack Kerouac is a weenie. All those
tributes to you and Snyder overflowing
the register—I couldn't stand it, what with your being
out of shape and hung over and not even making the top.
But today, sweating up switchback
after switchback from the shores of Ross Lake
through fog, through rain, through hail,
through drifts, through blow-downs and through
shredded boots, my hat is off to you in the wind
as I sit on the doorstep of your lookout,
gazing across the dam-drowned Skagit
to the darkness of Mox Peaks,
the ones described by Fred Beckey
as a good place for a funeral.
That's you, Jack. Your moxie to be up here
for two months and more before you died.
I was wrong: you're more than twice the man
I thought. The clouds are closing in again
and it's starting to snow. I'm out of here.

Deer at Twilight

Yesterday evening, from my campsite
in the forest on the edge of the reservoir,
I saw a deer walk cautiously to the end
of a long, sandy point. So far I was,
at first I thought it a coyote, or someone's dog,
or—who knows?—maybe a wolf.
But it was in fact a single deer,
diminished by distance, a silhouette
against the sheen. I could tell by the way
it held its head, innocently high and alert,
and the way it bent its neck to drink.
As twilight faded, I could not say
if it were standing on sand or water.
It was so quiet, the snowy peaks beyond
were bathed in such pure glow,
that had the deer walked all the way
across the lake, delicately
printing the surface with each fine hoof,
I would have bowed down and believed.

Little Beaver Creek

1.

A breeze is all:
little more than silence,
little less than hemlock
needles in air.

2.

Pale-green witch's hair
wisping down
from every limb of Douglas fir.
But where are all the bald witches?

3.

Mosquito, did you forget
to look at the calendar?
It's September, you know.

4.

Haggard cedars rise and rise above the creek,
looking down to watch their step.
At their feet, vine maple
gush crimson
whenever the old ones
stub their toes against the current.

5.

Shoots of alder lean out
from the sandy bank, floating
their arms in and above
the gray-green waters.

One yellow, scalloped leaf
circles the eddy on the surface,
little boat, marking the bend.

When the sun appears in the ripples,
even trees far in the forest
find a shimmer across their shade.

6.

Devil's club, why do you bother?
Along the trail, you keep extending
your fat hands like an over-friendly
greeter at the door of a church.

All you want is a fair shake,
but I'll slip into the sanctuary
while you're not looking.

7.

Nurse log, burrowed deep
in damp decay—
old mossy sow
with an infinite number of teats.

8.

Little seedling of silver fir,
reaching out in all directions,
where are you going, where
have you been, as you
stand up in your cradle?

9.

Red cedar, you wrap your roots
around the boulders at your base
as if you love them, as if
you will not let them go.
You have coated their little bottoms
with moss, a tender blanket,
tucked them in for another winter.

10.

High noon, and the sun
still hides behind the mountain.
Little valley, welcome
to the shades of autumn.

11.

Snowberries, pale-white
in a swift passage of rain,
are you getting ahead of yourselves?

12.

Nootka rose, I like your hips,
red-hot, the way
they sway
when I brush by.

13.

Prince's pine, your shriveled
flower brown as dust,
your little leaves
bereft upon the forest floor,
you are much too short
to be a pine—or a prince.
If I kiss you, will you
turn back into a frog?

14.

Coolwort, tiny earth-bound stars,
you are the only shining ones
in this dark forest among the berries.

15.

Mushroom in the middle of the trail,
do you mean to say
no one has come to see you this week?

16.

Banana slug, inquiring
the way with outstretched horns,
I love you for being living proof
that I am not the slowest
creature on this path.

17.

Tiny Pacific chorus frogs,
suddenly you appear at my feet,
leaping for joy. Could it be
you heard me singing from afar?

18.

The papery bulb
of a baldfaced hornet nest
hangs under a spray of hemlock.

Nearby, a spider web on tips of alder,
the big boy waiting in the center.

A passing hornet
smacks right into the web—
and bounces off, a shark too big for the net.

19.

Douglas squirrel, are you checking me out?
You are definitely checking me out.

20.

Black bear looking me in the eye,
be my guest. No, really.
That particular patch of huckleberries—
the one you are stripping clean
with your pink tongue?
I have zero interest in those berries.
Honest. They're yours.

Big Beaver Grove

(Thuja plicata)

It is quiet here, as it has been
for millennia among these giant cedar trees.
Somehow they make me quiet too,
and no longer damp and cold and tired,
as I step out of the vine maple and thimbleberry
where I have been singing
to entertain the bears in the brush.

For this is a place of sudden and enduring
silence, with only the hum of the creek below
and the faint splashing of stray drops
from the bend of cedar sprays
into the wide and waiting leaves
of devil's club and skunk cabbage.

These are the trees that just got lucky,
century after century. No fire, flood,
or avalanche has found this valley pocket yet,
and the roads and chainsaws never got this far.

House-sized boulders walled with ferns
and shingled with the deepest moss
dwell in and around these ancient ones,
these pillars tufted gray and old,
and queen's cup lilies and wild ginger
climb their trunks companionably,
as if wanting to see beyond the forest
floor, to put down roots in the sky.

In the Name of the Berry

(Sorbus scopulina)

The glory of the mountain ash in autumn
are the orange-red berries, flashing
forth in clusters that amaze the eye.

So delectable to say as well: *ash berry*.
Put them together: *ashberry*. That ought
to be a word, I think. It ought to be
a name, in fact, as resonant
as Emily Dickinson's *gingerbread*,
to which she raised her invisible hat.

And then I think, it *is* a word,
it *is* a name—the name of an actual poet,
of course. John Ashbery—the sound
of him the very secret of his success.

Here I am, coining a word
hundreds of years after its origin,
re-inventing the wheel of language,
discovering something I already knew.

Am I embarrassed? Not at all.
Each word of ours can be new
every morning, as full of mercy
as the gods. *Ashbery*—surely
a name to lift your cap to.

Could we but see, could we but hear
these words delicious on our tongues
and evanescent in the air,
we would be ever hat in hand,
bare-headed in dumb respect.

Oregon Grape (I)

(Mahonia nervosa)

Oregon grape, what makes you so sour today—
or every day, for that matter? Your blue berries,
ripe to bursting, look delicious but they're not.

Some native peoples would not eat them altogether.
Others, only intermixed with sweeter berries
from other plants—huckleberries, for example.

Are you jealous of your upland cousin,
thriving in subalpine meadows,
you stuck down here in the woods?

Listen: your little leaves in bending ladders,
dark green and shining like the holly,
lift me into holiday spirits. I'm serious.

With you it is Christmas in the gloom.
If you could just be happy about it,
I might forgive you for your flavor.

Sourdough Mountain Trail

(Goodyera oblongifolia)

Rattlesnake orchid, how glad I am
   your mottled scales uncoil
      themselves in stationary elegance,

the inflorescence of your fangs
   now, in fall, a brown bent stalk
      in foil to the rich blue berries of Oregon grape.

I touch the leather
   of your leaves like that imagined child
      at the hole of an adder.

I pass you by
   without the pause
      of a backward leap.

How peaceably you rest and grow beside the path,
   in all that you are,
      forsaking the menace of your name.

Dwarf dogood.   John

Pyramid Creek

Clearest stream, you wander here
   from gravel bed to gravel bed,
      napping in pools along the way.

You lave the roots of dusky cedars,
   leaning with age, and reassure them
      they have many years to leave.

Thick green moss describes your banks,
   saplings of hemlock, little hands
      of soft vine maple raised in air.

They want to ask if there is any other
   place you'd rather be, but off you go,
      down to the river, down to the sea.

Madrona on the San Juans

(Arbutus menziesii)

Madrona, that strip tease of yours
   is working again. The way you pearl
out of your bark, following your natural
   bent, turns my head in smooth surprise.
Your arms reach over the bay with longing,
   that supple skin, slightly sunburned,
blooming like a dusky rose.

Flushed

(Odocoileus hemionus)

Little deer, when you burst up
from that deep thicket of salal,
all in a flurry, at first I thought
you were another fat ruffed grouse.

When I stepped closer,
it was just your delicate head,
swiveling like a periscope
in a sea of green and leathery leaves.

Vine Maple (III)

(Acer circinatum)

Gray leaves, ghost leaves
   buried under
      the winter snowpack.

Now, in spring, they lay
   their desiccated hands
      atop the ladders

of Oregon grape,
   hoping to climb
      out of the grave.

Fairy Slipper

(Calypso bulbosa)

Growing singly
    out of the moss

on the forest floor,
    guarded by one grounded leaf,

you offer yourself to any
    who might try you on.

Pink satin foot-sole
    with a fringe,

who will hold you?
    Who will see you slip away?

Wood Violet

(Viola glabella)

Yellow wood violet,
   I don't deserve you.
      Does anyone?

The way you line
   both sides of the path
      above the creek,

leading upward
   from shade to sun,
      makes me think of you as

ushers to a new redemption.
   Each spring, a second chance.
      And a third. And a fourth.

Blow Down

(Betula papyrifera)

Paper birch, you are one of the only trees
    to cross this continent of ours.

But right now, all you are crossing
    is my trail, your prostrate trunk

about to publish on its scrolls
    a full account of all your travels.

Glacier Lily

(Erythronium grandiflorum)

Glacier lily, have you reappeared again—
    upside-down and facing the ground
        as if amazed the snow has fled?

Your six-fold petals curl in joy
    to have emerged from moss and stone,
        throwing up their yellow hands

like Pentecostal worshipers
    to praise the seed
        from which they came.

Oak Fern

(Gymnocarpium dryopteris)

Delicate is your understatement.
　　Frond within isosceles frond,
you clothe the steep and mossy bank
　　in loose and pendant plangency.

Lace is coarse beside
　　the tracings of your leaflets,
woven out of lime, of dew,
　　of thin green spiders in the breeze.

Horsetail

(Equisetum hyemale)

Little ancient forest of pipes,
the reed section of the Cascade orchestra,

you are as old as an instrument of nature
can be, counting back the endless codas.

Fossils put you in the pit
along with those Tchaikovsky-loving

dinosaurs, stomping out their tympani,
marching to their own bassoons.

Dwarf Dogwood

(Cornus canadensis)

You? Dwarf? Is that why you are climbing
   the bark of this Douglas fir,
      checking your height in a mirror of cloud
         with each green blossom?

Your four leaves and your four sepals,
   not to mention your four petals,
      make you the perfect Jungian flower,
         a tetrameter poem to the eye.

Climb on, stout heart. Or rest awhile.
   Who needs to be tall when you can refresh
      yourself in the rain north-south-east-west,
         the sum and center of every compass?

Western Trillium (I)

(Trillium ovatum)

Trillium, you mean spring business.
No sleight-of-hand in a slender shadow
like a fairy slipper for you, no ground-shy

plume of Oregon grape—you stalk
your presence, open your full throat
to the wind, pistils drawn to face the sun.

White like a blouse, white like
a fresh and open page, you shoulder
into publication, letting us know

just how to read the morning news,
how to see what's written upon
those three green leaves about your waist.

Bleeding Heart

(Dicentra formosa)

Finally, a flower after my own.
   You there, hanging

in unashamed bivalve clusters
   at the feet of ancient cedars.

So few of them left, you know.
   Is that what breaks you? Is that

what makes you wear your sweet pink
   ventricles on your green sleeve?

Hooker's Fairy Bell

(Disporum hookeri)

Fairy bell, you seem to like it
here in the shade, your lanterns hung
in pairs, knee-high, to light the pathway
if they could. Hooker's you may be,
but you glow white, not red,
to mark this district of the forest.

If I am not mistaken, you were named
in deference to an English botanist
who never made the trip to see you.
When the fairies bring us gold,
it is a secret we must keep.
But I am a richer man than he.

Chocolate Lily

(Fritillaria affinia)

Chocolate lily, why are you
the only one I've seen so far?

Of all flavors, you are my favorite;
that alone might make you rare.

I could eat you up in a moment,
much as a llama I once knew

devoured a whole huge Washington lily
in the very instant we said,

Look! How pretty—

Candy Flower

(Claytonia sibirica)

Candy flower, your leaves reach up
    like spoons to taste that peppermint.

Your other name is Siberian miner's lettuce,
    but who would want the gulag

of such pale fare?
    You belong with the chocolate lily,

or next to a bed of vanilla leaf,
    where you could think of opening shop.

As well you should, for a forest
    sweet in tooth and claw.

Starry Solomon's Plume

(Maianthemum stellatum)

Starry, starry Solomon's plume,
your constellations float

in clusters lowly wise,
zig-zagging asterisks of light,

reminding thick and shaggy cedars,
though they breach the nether skies,

that even smallest things may be
arrayed on earth as they are in heaven.

Corral Lake

Mosquitoes hum & hum & hum.
　　But spring-green larch

in morning light.
　　The call of a robin.

The silence of a golden cornice
　　hung like an earring on the pass.

Nohokomeen Glacier

Nohokomeen, what do you mean
    by your pillowed icefall in the sun,
        slow-sleeping in your scissored bowl?

My trail will not take me where
    you shift and flow, where you become
        the creek that dreams your legacy.

But I travel you with the eye
    from below, passing your peace,
        hoping your deeps will long endure.

Applegate Paintbrush

(Castilleja applegatei)

Did you paint the sunrise
    over on Jackita Ridge?

If so, you forgot
    to wash the tips

of every one of
    your bracts and blossoms.

Panicled Bluebells

(Mertensia paniculata)

Bluebells, when I finally
   reach a tiny stream
in the crease of the mountainside,
   you are waiting in your campanile,
ringing the changes of my steps.

Wild Strawberry

(Fragaria diorcus)

These strawberry fields, if not forever,
   will last for a spring and a summer.

Facing the sun on this high ridge,
   they grow exactly where they will—

no tractored rows, no children
   filling their broken baskets.

Just a visiting bear or two when time is ripe—
   something, should you round the bend

upon this slope some evening,
   that will give you pause.

Sitka Mountain Ash

(Sorbus sitchensis)

Mountain ash, I was so taken
　　by your berries, orange and scarlet
　　　　in the fall, that I forgot about

your umbeled inflorescence.
　　You reach your flat white floral
　　　　crowns like plates of china

over the folds of each ravine,
　　your leaves a setting of green
　　　　silver for every serving.

Cow Parsnip

(Heracleum maximum)

Cow parsnip, most clumsy and bovine
of herbs and flowers, here you are
in the pasture of an avalanche track,

domesticating the mountains again,
just as you do in Siberia, where
the Russian peasants call you *pushki*,

because, I guess, you are that
insistent, a stubborn Holstein
shouldering her way to the trough.

Fanleaf Cinquefoil

(Potentilla flabellifolia)

Cinquefoil, can you dance a cinquepace
like Sir Andrew Aguecheek?

Or is your gift in the
tongues of your yellow petals,

presented like ungartered stockings
to each fool who stirs this way?

Your leaves give fanfare
to each afternoon's performance

on this globe. Play on.
I am your eager groundling.

Serviceberry

(Amelanchier alnifolia)

As if that is what sustained old Robert
    on his way to the Klondike,
its blossoms rhyming white in spring
    but fading in fall
to berries of black doggerel.

Douglas Fir

(Pseudotsuga menziesii)

Douglas fir, there's something so normal
    about you. Your straight, stout limbs,
        your furrowed bark, your needles
            basking in the ordinary sun.

You gain your girth without our ever noticing.
    Yet here you are, invisible,
        dropping your cones
            that fit so neatly in the hand.

Arrowleaf Balsamroot

(Balsamorhiza sagittata)

Balsamroot, wide-eyed and turning
to the light, your open blossoms,

even in this clouded noon, blink
welcome to each stony switchback.

And your leaves, those
fulsome arrows, pointing the way.

Racer

(Coluba constrictor)

Racer, you erase yourself
    when I step near.

The first I know, you've flung
    a fluid curve of tail,

that olive muscle,
    down the rocky mountainside

in a matter of course,
    a maze of motion.

Deer Bones

Funny how the inside of a femur
looks just like sponge cake.
But bones to dust and dust to soil
and soil to seed and seed to stalk
and stalk to grain and grain to meal,
I will eat that cake someday, that
sponge cake with the frosting of death.

Death Camas

(Toxicordion venenosum)

I saw you in a misplaced
   grove of ponderosa
      under Desolation Peak,

then learned your name
   on the dry south shore
      of an island in the Salish Sea.

And though I did not place
   my tongue within
      your creamy inflorescence,

I knew one day
   that I would take communion
      with your bitter oils.

Western Trillium (II)

(Trillium ovatum)

Trillium, like a spawning salmon
you turn red before you die,

an emblem of your sacrifice
for what comes next:

all for the seed, all for
the silver fin of a petal.

October Light

(Charmerion augustifolium)

Whitespun seeds of fireweed
   come floating down the mountainside
      past frosted backs
         of brown-bent bracken,
            crimson reach of huckleberry.

Magenta blossoms give short way
   to flaming leaves and then to ash,
      swirling now like snowflakes
         on a winter morning,
            last breath of a sunlit storm.

Pearly Everlasting

(Anaphalis margaritacea)

Are you really? Underneath the snows
of winter, do you blossom on and on?
Do the pocket gophers crave you,
tunneling beneath that blanket,
pray to enter your secret chambers,
rest inside your open gates?

I see your flowering, fruiting
clusters, hanging on into October,
leaning into the open path,
making way, ushering whatever is holy
into the presence of things that stay.

winter birches

Thunder Creek

Salmonberry blossoms nod pink and shy
   on the April shore, and the creek courses,
      not thunderously, but with the murmur
         of ongoing news, a secret of sorts.

The elderly cedars looking on
   are most certainly in on it. So too
      the vine maple, coming into light green leaf.

It has something to do with snow up high,
   we down low, drinking it in.

Vine Maple (I)

(Acer circinatum)

Up and at 'em, *circinatum.*
    And you are, twisting
your gauntlet over the path,
    a vernal tunnel of morning light—
our whole story the understory.

Any minute we expect a shining
    couple around the bend,
treading the carpet of old leaf-fall,
    what's left behind when snows
and differences have melted.

False Solomon's Seal

(Mainthemum racemosa)

False Solomon's seal, you trade
    in frankincense and myrhh,
        filling the forest with your fragrance.

There is a wisdom in the ladder
    of your leaves, clasping their way
        to each perfusion of scent and blossom.

Multiplied beneath the sunlit spaciousness
    of Douglas fir, you make a Milky Way
        of stars, as if the skies had poured

themselves into our lap, born
    again as a field of flowers, one vast aroma,
        calling us to a true home.

Forget-Me-Not

(Myosotis laxa)

The name, perhaps, of every creature,
not just this one-in-a-crowd of small blue faces
at my feet on the edge of an April campground.

Even the syntax sends us back to those forgotten
but who never wished to be. Not "don't forget me"
but, rather, "forget me not," like someone
out of *Hamlet* or the King James version of Job.

And, notice, not stated in hope but in fear.
"Remember me" would imply some expectation
of follow-through. But the plaintive appeal
"forget me not" assumes the flower is not worthy
of remembrance, and if not remembered,
not known, and if not known, hardly
to have existed at all, hardly to have had a self.

In my freshman year of college, once a week
I tutored a boy in the basement of a downtown church.
His face was the beauty of dark chocolate.
Once we went on a camping trip and found
a raccoon and her litter in the hollow of a tree.

When night came, he did not want to return
to that hollow. At the end of the year,
after our last session, he said, "Do not forget me.
Don't forget me." His name was Clayton.
I'm pretty sure his name was Clayton.

Round One

(Dryocopus pileatus)

Just now, a pileated woodpecker piled
his red pileum right into the sliding glass door
and then retreated to the trunk of a Douglas fir.

A collision like that would put most any other bird
on its back, claws up for a KO. But the woodpecker,
being a woodpecker, with a skull as crushable
as an anvil and a brain like a rubber paddle-ball,
just seems to shrug it off, perhaps convinced
that his rival reflection in the window
has finally met his nemesis
in a furious jousting match in the skies.

On his vertical perch, the woodpecker appears,
well, pileated, a bit ruffled along the crest,
but from this angle he sees no sign
of his Narcissus-like opponent.
And, perhaps, he misses him.

Panther Creek

Panther Creek, your flow beneath
the highway bridge does not compare
to that between these hemlock,
cedar, and Douglas fir, not to mention
the alder slotted into your current.

Of course, there is less of you
the higher we climb, but a creek
is so much more itself
apart from the combustive talk
of cars and trucks and things that go
away before they think to arrive.

It has something to do with your mossy
cliffs, the turquoise tumble of your waters—
even the nettles along your bank,
nettlesome as they may be.

Most of all I like the way
you speak to us in your own language,
saying, and then saying again,
what comes naturally.

Sauk Mountain Eagle

(Haliateetus leucocephalus)

From my perch on the shoulder of Sauk Mountain,
I see an eagle rising and rising,
its head and tail feathered white against the sun.

It is far above the Skagit now, looking
not for salmon but for meadow creatures
like ourselves on a lazy Sunday afternoon—

the pair of toddlers herding fuzzy caterpillars
while their mothers pause on the trail,
the young man taking time to pose

his girlfriend in a wind-teased dress,
the octogenarian couples shuffling amiably
down the path, letting their conversation glide.

It is hard not to feel superintended
by this eagle, our chosen icon, and, in turn,
in watching it circle over our heads,

to see, not ourselves anymore, but simply
the eagle, its literal aloofness among us,
the way it gathers all things into its eye.

To see the eagle is, for a moment,
to be the eagle—a hint of how the Indians did it,
gaining their totems, finding themselves

both here and somewhere in the sky.

Bridge Creek Trail

(Pteridium aquilinum)

As if they have been lynched by winter,
brown corpses of bracken fern
hang limp from the bare branches
of slide alder. The snow just left.

Greening and blooming underfoot
are the upstarts: wood violet, glacier
lily, salmonberry, bleeding heart.

But the dangling, desiccated
bodies want to be heard.
We were here, they would say—
last summer, we grew head high.
Just because you are living,
they will come for you.

Bear Story

(Ursus americanus)

Late afternoon, I'm ten miles down Bridge Creek,
footsore, carrying on a conversation in my head
with the ranger who has just cancelled
the artist-in-residence program.
I am posing another masterful question
before the crowd when suddenly,
on the trail below me, *zip! zam!*
two black bear cubs rocket up
the narrow trunk of a Douglas fir.
I make the connection. I scan the base
of the Doug fir. And there, rising to full height,
is the cinnamon mama in all her glory,
not thirty yards away. So, I think,
the artist-in-residence himself
is about to suffer cancellation.
But the bear, big and jowly enough,
appears more confused than anything,
like a grumpy, overweight professor
looking up from his thirty-year-old lecture notes
with a dim awareness that someone in the upper tier
has made a disparaging comment.
Then the professor returns
to his main point, and so too the bear
goes back to munching spring-green serviceberry.
The cubs get the all-clear and climb
back down to their desks, while I
leave the classroom, of course,
doing a slow about-face
and tip-toeing up several switchbacks
until I can see from a safer distance,
downwind. For most of an hour they forage
patiently by the path, and I watch their napes
of fur in the bushes, wondering if
I'll ever get a chance to descend.
Finally they amble off, and I shoulder
my pack and I sing, I sing, so artfully,
all the way down the trail.

Buckner Orchard

To live among dogwoods and Canada geese,
tending a grove of small, hardy apples—
well, you could do worse. Add a broad pasture
in the bend of a river—fir, maple, cedar, cottonwood
lining its banks—and you start to get the picture.

True, you have to barge in most of your hay
from down-lake because of all the bracken
in the back forty, but the three-mile ride
to the landing is its own kind of pleasure.

In spring and summer you hear the shout
of a waterfall across the valley.
It says, *I'll stay, whether you do or not.*

Twinflower

(Linnaea borealis)

Who would guess, with your pair
of downcast, blousy blossoms

so close to your matted leaves,
that you are actually a shrub?

No hiding in these bushes.
But you bank the berm

of this irrigation ditch
in the forest, witness to water

hurrying from creek to orchard.
At least there are two of you,

every time—for each fork
in the channel, a second opinion.

Oregon Grape (II)

(Mahonia nervosa)

You blossoming fool. Last I saw you
in the fall, you were bent to the ground
with sour blue berries.

Now, in spring,
you raise your racemes, garish yellow,
to the air, ready to start all over again.

For what? I ask you.
Like a child, you insist on the same story,
over and over, even though you know

the ending—your powdery bloom
a delight to the eye, another
betrayal to the tongue.

O Western White

(Pinus monticola)

O western white, your pine cones
are the big bananas of the forest.
Which puts me in mind, not that you'd
be interested, of a friend who told me
about an ad for washing machines
on the television in Seattle.
We've slashed our prices!
said the bouncing salesman.
Only two hundred bananas,
and you can take one out the door!
Wouldn't you know it, someone
took him at his word and brought
two hundred ripe bananas into the store.
It went to court. The customer won.
Which goes to show, O western white,
you do not know how rich you may be.

Snag

(Pinus contorta)

When a lodgepole succumbs
to the snow and the wind and leans out
over a lake, dipping its branch tips
into the water, the trunk will lose
its roughcast bark and turn
white and smooth in an afterlife
of moon and sun. And before
the ants have completed their work,
dusting the waves with the last
of their indigestible powders,
the trunk will abrade to a gossamer
surface of fine white hairs—
fine as the silk on the head of a child,
as the wispy down above the lip
of a grandmother, bent with age.

Walking on Water, Pyramid Lake

These particular bugs can do it,
dimpling the surface with their feet,
and no one has built a church in their name.

Other bugs swim underwater with abandon,
with no blue ribbons to show for it.
That leaves the rest of us to perform
our daily miracles without applause.

This rock, for example, sheared flat
by who knows what torturous force,
left to host its lime-green share

of crustose lichen, that concoction
of algae and fungi which long ago,
not even listening to Rodney King,
decided we can get along if we just try.

Lines Written While Gazing up the Easton Glacier

Mt. Baker, you're looking like a whole lot
of ice cream right now, at least two scoops
of vanilla, smoothed together in what could be
the best sundae ever made. I mean, you look
truly delicious, reminding me of the crush
I had on lovely Leslie Easton in the fifth grade.

I want to provide your chocolate topping,
drizzling the sauce of my boot-prints
all the way from bowl to summit, and then
I'll be your cherry too, if that's what you want.

I could spoon each side of you with the curve
of my adze before you melt—and if I had to,
I would share, since someone
in the last few years forgot to put you
back in the freezer and left you here
on top of the oven, still warming.

The Man Who Pushed a Mountain into the Fire

He wasn't that strong, actually.
But when lightning struck,
and the trees caught, he saw
the mountain would have to go.

It was mostly made of yellow
pumice, the kind of rock that floats
on water, so that helped.

Still, it took some sweat,
and a short prayer, before
the slope began to give,
more out of politeness than anything.

And then he was able to walk
away, his fingertips a little dusky,
as if to remind him of his effort,
what it had taken to save
himself, what sacrificed.

How the North Cascades Almost Changed the Outcome of the Civil War

The Picket Range in the North Cascades
is named for its resemblance to a picket fence,
not in remembrance of the soldier
George E. Pickett, who in fact was posted
to Fort Bellingham in 1856. But at my age,
to try to climb most any of the Picket summits,
much less have a go at the entire Picket Traverse,
would be as good an enterprise
as Pickett's Charge at Gettysburg in 1863.

Had General Pickett looked up across
those fields to the Union lines
behind that long, stone-angled fence
and thought of the Pickets he might once
or twice have seen from a forested hilltop
somewhere above Puget Sound or from
the deck of a ship in the Strait of Juan de Fuca,
and had he known the future names
of those strange peaks—Terror, Fury,
Challenger—and of the peaks so near at hand—
Despair, Damnation, Desolation,
Formidable, Forbidden, Torment—

might he have paused, might he
at least have hesitated, before
he sent wave after wave of grim, gray men
against those hopeless alder thickets,
those tangled swamps of devil's club,
those jagged glaciers thundering
into the deep dark cirques below,
that granite line of bayonets
bristling upward into an ever-smoking sky?

Pacific Crest Trail

Mystical thread of footprints from Canada
to Mexico—the direction Eric Ryback came,
my high school hero, supposedly the first
to make it all the way. Except he didn't,
having accepted a ride or two on the dusty
maze of logging roads beneath Mt. Shasta.

But he started out bravely enough,
an eighty-pound pack in May, arresting
himself time and again with an ice ax
on those snowy traverses all across
the North Cascades. For a while there
I thought of following in his steps,
but then the peaks began to call,
and the golden trail merely became
something to cross en route to a summit.

Still, whenever I do find myself on the PCT
for a day or so—on Muir Pass in the Sierra,
or Soda Mountain in the Siskiyous—
I feel the pull, the continuity of the thing,
the possibility of putting one scuffed boot
in front of the other. Never mind
that I'm pushing sixty, that my right knee
has decided to ache, that my pack
gets heavier every year. The path unrolls
illimitably in answer to our infinite longing,
every blaze a terrestrial promise, every switch-
back a return to a yet more excellent way.

Sustainability

(Laryx lyallis)

A few weeks after my mother died,
I dreamed that she was waiting for me
in a ravine of spring-green larches.
There was no worry in her eyes, and
she sat there with her knees drawn up,
content to be in the filtered sunlight.
Funny, because she never lived
among larch trees—my mom grew up
on an orange grove and raised us
in the Douglas fir. I do not live
among them either, apart from my rare
visits to the North Cascades. But when
I'm here, as now I am, sitting barefoot
on Cutthroat Pass among amber larches
bathing every bowl and basin,
I have a sense that she's okay,
and that I am too, born to witness what
I can within this green and golden world
which still persists, with or without us—
but mostly with us, I've come to believe.
Things and people pass away,
but that's when they become themselves.
There's a new heaven, a new earth,
around and about us—and not much
different from the better parts of the old.
We don't live there very often,
but when we do, eternity
ignites in a moment, light in the larches
that shines. And shines.

Image Lake

(Charadrius vociferous)

One evening at Image Lake,
    a killdeer swung across the surface
        in lovely spurts, unaware
            of the reflection of the dark

subalpine firs, churchly and steepled
    on every hand, and also cleanly unaware
        of the radiance of Glacier Peak,
            its icy presence in the waters.

The killdeer may have clearly seen
    whatever it was searching for
        as insects circled in the last of golden light,
            and perhaps, for an instant, even knew

its flight was not just one but two,
    perfectly mirrored as it crossed,
        in all its gainly, rocking form,
            from one far shore to the other.

THANKS

Almost all of the poems in this book were drafted during a pair of residencies in fall 2014 and spring 2015 in the North Cascades of Washington State—the first with North Cascades National Park and the second with the North Cascades Institute. I wish to thank the rangers and staff of these organizations for their very helpful support and direction during my weeks and months with them. I am especially indebted to Rowena Watson of the park and Katie Roloson of the institute. Many mountain days to you both!

I have also traveled many happy miles in the North Cascades with my good friend Chris Norment, an amazing field biologist and a very fine writer to boot, and with my beautiful wife, Sharon— always inspiring, almost always ahead of me.

In addition, I thank my provost, Mark Sargent, at Westmont College for granting me a sabbatical on which to pursue something other than grading papers and standing in front of a classroom (not that those are bad things, on a good day). I deeply appreciate his support, and that of my many students and colleagues.

Finally, I wish to thank my poet friends in and around Santa Barbara who have had a hand in editing a good many of these poems: Marsha de la O, Perie Longo, Glenna Luschei, John Ridland, Bruce Schmidt, David Starkey, Phil Taggart, and Chryss Yost. Without your eyes and ears, this book would be a shambling thing.

ACKNOWLEDGMENTS

Iba: "Oak Fern" and "Panicled Bluebells"

Archaeopteryx: "Sauk Mountain Eagle"

Ascent: "Huckleberry Love Poem" and "Snag"

Askew: "Wild Strawberry"

Blue Unicorn: "Death Camas" and "Vine Maple (I)"

Blueline: "Fanleaf Cinquefoil," "October Light," and "Wood Violet"

Books & Culture: "The Thing That Is Not"

Cascadia Review: "Fairy Slipper" and "Sitka Mountain Ash"

Chattermarks: "Pyramid Creek"

Christian Century: "Bleeding Heart," "False Solomon's Seal,"
    "Oregon Grape (I)," "Pearly Everlasting," "Starry
    Solomon's Plume," "Twinflower," and "Vine Maple (III)"

Cirque: "O Western White"

Cloudbank: "Western Trillium (I)"

Comstock Review: "Madrona on the San Juans" and "Thunder Creek"

Curator: "Sustainability"

Hummingbird: "Applegate Paintbrush"

Into the Teeth of the Wind: "Crater Mountain"

Kentucky Review: "Desolation Peak" and "Dry Creek"

Kerf: "Horsetail" and "Western Trillium (II)"

Leaping Clear: "Bridge Creek Trail"

Noon: "Racer" and "Serviceberry"

Nourish: "Flushed"

Packinghouse Review: "Flyaway"

Ruminate: "Buckner Orchard"

Soundings Review: "Deer at Twilight"

Spectrum: "Corral Lake," "In the Name of the Berry" and "Round One"

Terrene: "Forget-Me-Not"

Triggerfish Critical Review: "Devils Park Shelter," "How the
    North Cascades Almost Changed the Outcome of the
    Civil War," and "Pacific Crest Trail"

Whale Road Review: "Deer Bones"

Windfall: "Big Beaver Grove"

Written River: "Little Beaver Creek"

You Are Here: "Panther Creek"

"Sustainability" has also appeared in *Between Midnight and
    Dawn* (Paraclete Press).

"Wood Violet" has also appeared in *The Turning Aside*
    (Cascade Books).

ABOUT THE AUTHOR

Paul J. Willis is the author of four previous collections of poetry, the most recent of which is *Getting to Gardisky Lake*. He has also published a four-part eco-fantasy novel, *The Alpine Tales*, and two collections of creative nonfiction, most recently *To Build a Trail: Essays on Curiosity, Love, and Wonder*. He is a professor of English at Westmont College and a former poet laureate of Santa Barbara, California. Learn more at www.pauljwillis.com.

CPSIA information can be obtained
at www.ICGtesting.com
Printed in the USA
FSHW01n1751200618
49562FS